Academic
Learning
Series

Networking
Essentials
Second Edition

Lab Manual

Microsoft *Press*

PUBLISHED BY
Microsoft Press
A Division of Microsoft Corporation
One Microsoft Way
Redmond, Washington 98052-6399

Library of Congress Cataloging-in-Publication Data
Networking Essentials, Second Edition: Academic Learning Series / Microsoft Corporation.
    p. cm.
  Includes index.
  ISBN 1-57231-527-X
  ISBN 1-57231-909-7 (Academic Learning Series)
  1. Computer networks--Programmed instruction. I. Microsoft Corporation.
TK5105.5.N4669 1997
513.2--dc21
                                      97-34595
                                        CIP

Printed and bound in the United States of America.

4 5 6 7 8 9 WCWC   3 2 1 0 9

Distributed in Canada by ITP Nelson, a division of Thomson Canada Limited.

A CIP catalogue record for this book is available from the British Library.

Microsoft Press books are available through booksellers and distributors worldwide. For further information about international editions, contact your local Microsoft Corporation office, or contact Microsoft Press International directly at fax (425) 936-7329. Visit our Web site at mspress.microsoft.com.

BackOffice, Microsoft, Microsoft Press, MS, MS-DOS, Visual Basic, Windows, the Windows logo, and Windows NT are registered trademarks and MSN is a trademark of Microsoft Corporation.

Other product and company names mentioned herein may be the trademarks of their respective owners.

Acquisitions Editor: William Setten
Series Editor: Barbara Moreland

Part No. 097-0002061

Introduction to Lab Exercises

Included with the Academic Learning Series (ALS) texts are hands-on lab exercises designed to give you practical experience using Microsoft Windows NT 4.0. This hands-on experience is an essential part of your training because it is difficult to truly understand and use the operating system and its features without having had the opportunity to explore firsthand the menus, options, and responses. The tasks included in these exercises provide an opportunity for you to test the concepts presented in the text, to use Microsoft Windows NT's utilities and tools, and to explore the structure of Microsoft Windows NT's operating system.

The lab exercises are best used in a classroom setting, though some exercises can be completed individually. The exercises presume a classroom network setup in one or more Windows NT domains with shared resources (depending upon the specific ALS text being used).

The directory of subdirectories, programs, and data files designed to support these labs can be shared from the instructor's system or installed on each student's system. A lab setup guide is provided for the instructor to use in setting up the classroom to support the labs.

The lab exercises do not precisely mirror the text's practice activities. Domain names, user names, IP addresses, shared resources, and other specific references in the lab exercises may be somewhat different from similar references in the ALS text or from those used in setting up the classroom network.

Local constraints must be followed to ensure proper network operations. Since it is not possible to predict each institution's local networking requirements, your instructor will explain differences that occur.

The old saying "The way to get to Carnegie Hall is to practice, practice, practice" is equally true of the pursuit of personal competency and Microsoft Certification. The tests required for Microsoft Certified Product Specialist, Systems Engineer, or other Microsoft certifications are demanding. One of the best ways to become confident in the use of Microsoft Windows NT is to complete each of the assigned lab exercises as well as the practice tasks included in the text.

Lab 1: Log On to the Network

Objectives

After completing this lab, you will be able to:

■   Log on to the Classroom1 domain network.

Estimated time to complete this lab: 10 minutes

Exercise 1
Log on to the Classroom1 Domain Network

In this exercise, you will learn how to log on to the Classroom1 domain to access your server's resources. You have been provided with a student account, named **Studentx**, to use to log in to the network.

➤   **To log on to the Classroom1 domain**

1. Start your Windows NT 4.0 Server.

2. When the **Begin Logon** dialog box reappears, press CTRL-ALT-DELETE to display the **Login Information** dialog box.

3. Type **Studentx** as the User name and press TAB.

4. Type **password** as the Password and press ENTER or click **OK**.

   You should now be logged in as the Studentx user. If this does not work, repeat the steps above or ask your instructor for help. If you are having difficulty, remember to check the spelling of the User name; although it is not case-sensitive, the specific characters must be typed correctly, including the hyphen included in the name and the numerical digits at the end of the name. Also, remember that the password is case-sensitive and must be typed as **password** in lower-case letters.

Lab 2: Using Windows NT Diagnostics to View System Information

Objectives

After completing this lab, you will be able to:

- Define the hardware and software resources installed on a Windows NT system.
- Create a diagnostic report.

Exercise 1
Using Windows NT Diagnostics to View Configuration Information

In this exercise, you will use WinMSD to view configuration information for your Windows NT 4.0 Server.

➤ **To view software configuration information**

1. Log on to your computer as Student*x*, where *x* is the number assigned to you for this class.

2. Click the **Start** button, point to **Programs**, point to **Administrative Tools (Common)**, and then click **Windows NT Diagnostics**.

3. Locate the following information by reviewing the tabs in the Windows NT Diagnostics window. In the following table, record the name of the tab and the value for the information requested in the following table.

Answers recorded in the table will vary for each student.

Requested information	Tab	Value
Registered owner	*Version*	*Administrator*
Registered organization	*Version*	*@ CLI*
Version number	*"*	*4.0 (Build ...)*
Build number	*"*	*1381*
System root (windir)	*Environment*	*D:\WINNT*
Domain name	*Network*	*Domain09*
CPU type	*System*	*Intel 880*

4. Locate the following information, and then record the value of the information requested in the following table.

Answers recorded in the table will vary for each student.

Requested information	Your configuration
Total physical memory	*130,484 K*
Available physical memory	*103,280*
Total page file space	*131,072*
Available page file space	*131,072*
Paging files	*pagefile.sys*

Exercise 2
Saving a Windows NT Diagnostics Report

In this exercise, you will save a Windows NT Diagnostics report for your computer, and then view the report.

➤ **To create a Windows NT Diagnostics report**

1. On the **File** menu, click **Save Report**.

   The **Create Report** dialog box appears.

2. Under **Scope**, click **All tabs**.

3. Under **Detail Level**, click **Complete**.

4. Click **OK**.

   The **Save WinMSD Report** dialog box appears.

5. Save the file as **C:\Msdrpt.txt**.

   The **Generating WinMSD Report** dialog box appears, containing a status bar indicating the current progress.

6. Click **OK** to exit Windows NT Diagnostics.

➤ **To read a Windows NT Diagnostics report**

1. Start Windows NT Explorer, and then click drive C.

2. Double-click **Msdrpt.txt** to view your report.

   Notepad starts, and then displays the Msdrpt.txt file.

3. On the **Search** menu, click **Find**, and then in Msdrpt.txt, the NT Diagnostics report you just created, locate the following information.

Requested information	System configuration
PROCESSOR_ARCHITECTURE	x86
PROCESSOR_LEVEL	6
PROCESSOR_IDENTIFIER	x86 family 6 Model 5
PROCESSOR_REVISION → 0502	Stepping 2, Genuine Intel

4. OPTIONAL: If a printer is available in your classroom, print the report.

5. Close Notepad, and then close Windows NT Explorer.

Lab 3: Displaying Network and I/O Settings

Objectives

After completing this lab, you will be able to:

- Display Network Card and Protocol Properties.
- Display Programmable Interrupt (IRQ) and Memory Settings.

Estimated time to complete this lab: 20 minutes

Exercise 1
Displaying Network Adapter Card and Protocol Properties

In this exercise, you will use the Network Properties dialog box to display the current system network settings, including the name and resources for the adapter card, the protocol(s) installed, and other information.

➤ **To display Network Properties**

1. Log on to your computer as Student*x*, where *x* is the number assigned to you for this class.

2. Using the mouse, point to **Network Neighborhood** and right-click to display the menu.

3. Click **Properties** to display network properties.

Note You may also use the Network program icon in the Control Panel to display this same dialog box.

4. Use the indicated tabs to enter the information in the tables below. Although only a single adapter and protocol is expected, your computer may have additional settings.

Answers recorded in the tables will vary for each student.

Identification tab

Computer name:	*Student 09*
Domain name:	*Domain 09*

Adapters tab

Network adapter:	*(1) GT 2500 III PCI Ethernet Adapter*

On the **Adapters** Tab, click the **Properties**… button.

Adapter IRQ:	*11*
Port address:	*E410 - E41F*

Protocols tab

Protocol(s):	*NWLink IPX/SPX Compatible Transport*
	NWLink NetBios
	TCP/IP Protocol

Exercise 2
Using Windows NT Diagnostics to View Network and IRQ Information

In this exercise, you will use WinMSD to view configuration information for your Windows NT 4.0 Server.

➤ **To view configuration information**

1. Log on to your computer as Student*x*, where *x* is the number assigned to you for this class.

2. Click the **Start** button, point to **Programs**, point to **Administrative Tools (Common)**, and then click **Windows NT Diagnostics**.

3. Locate the following information by displaying the **Resources** tab in the Windows NT Diagnostics window. Record the information about IRQs in the table below.

Answers recorded in the table will vary for each student.

Requested information	Assigned to
IRQ 0	N/A
IRQ 1	i8042 prt
IRQ 2	N/A
IRQ 3	Serial
IRQ 4	Serial
IRQ 5	
IRQ 6	Floppy
IRQ 7	
IRQ 8	
IRQ 9	
IRQ 10	
IRQ 11	RTL 8029
IRQ 12	i8042 prt
IRQ 13	
IRQ 14	atapi
IRQ 15	

4. Locate the following information by displaying the **Network** tab in the Windows NT Diagnostics window. Record the information in the table below.

Answers recorded in the table will vary for each student.

Requested information	Value
Your access level	Admin & Local
Workgroup or domain	DOMAIN 09
Network version	4.0
LanRoot	DOMAIN 09
Logged-on users	1
Current user (1)	Administrator
Logon domain	DOMAIN 09
Logon server	Student 09

Lab 4: Configuring TCP/IP

Objectives

After completing this lab, you will be able to:

- Manually configure TCP/IP parameters on a computer running Windows NT.
- Use Ping to verify IP connectivity.
- Use IPCONFIG to verify the IP settings.
- (Optional) Automatically configure TCP/IP by using DHCP.

Before You Begin

Before beginning this lab, your instructor should assign each student an IP address to be used in this lab. Record your assigned IP address below.

_____._____._____._____

Use your assigned IP address to replace the *w.x.y.z* placeholder in the lab.

This lab assumes that the Instructor computer has an IP address of 131.107.2.200. If it is different, your instructor will tell you, and you should substitute the correct address for the Instructor computer, where appropriate, throughout this lab.

Estimated time to complete this lab: 20 minutes

Exercise 1
Manually Configuring TCP/IP on a Computer Running Windows NT 4.0

In this exercise, you will manually configure the TCP/IP parameters on a computer running Windows NT.

Note   Installing a Network Protocol will require access to the Windows NT Server 4.0 installation files; for an Intel-based system, this is the \I386 directory shared on the \\Instructor*x* system or on the Windows NT Server 4.0 CD.

➤ **To manually configure TCP/IP**

1. Log on as Administrator.

2. Right-click **Network Neighborhood**, then click **Properties**.

   The **Network** dialog box appears.

3. Click the **Protocols** tab.

4. Click **Add**.

   The **Select Network Protocols** dialog box appears.

5. Click **TCP/IP Protocol**, and then click **OK**.

   The **TCP/IP Setup** dialog box appears.

6. Click **No** to indicate that you are *not* using DHCP at this time.

7. Type the correct path to your Windows NT Server 4.0 installation directory and then click continue.

8. When the setup is complete, click **Close**.

9. The Microsoft **TCP/IP Properties** dialog box appears showing the **IP Address** tab. Click **Specify an IP address**, and then enter the following information.

In this box...	Use...	
IP Address	131.107.2.200	(Unless instructed otherwise)
Subnet Mask	255.255.255.0	(Unless instructed otherwise)
Default Gateway	Leave blank	(Unless instructed otherwise)

10. Click **OK**.

A **System Process—System Error** dialog box appears, displaying the following message:

```
The system has detected an IP address conflict with another system on
the network. The local interface has been disabled. More details are
available in the system event log. Consult your network administrator
to resolve the conflict.
```

Why does this message appear?

_____

11. Click **OK**.

➤ **To specify a correct address**

1. In the **Network** dialog box, click the **Protocols** tab.

2. Click **TCP/IP Protocol**, and then click **Properties**.

3. Click the **IP Address** tab, click **Specify an IP address**, and then enter the following information.

In this box...	Use...	
IP Address	*w.x.y.z*	This is the address supplied to you by your instructor. It will be in the form 131.107.2.*x*, where *x* is your student number. (Unless instructed otherwise)
Subnet Mask	255.255.255.0	(Unless instructed otherwise)
Default Gateway	Leave blank	(Unless instructed otherwise)

4. Click **OK** to close the **Properties** dialog box.

5. Click **OK** to close the **Network** dialog box.

6. Shut down and restart Windows NT Server.

Exercise 2
Using Ping to Verify IP Connectivity

In this exercise, you will use Ping to verify that the TCP/IP configuration is correct.

➤ **To test and verify that the TCP/IP configuration is correct**

1. Log on as Administrator.

2. Start a Command Prompt.

3. To test that IP is working and bound to your adapter, type **ping 127.0.0.1** and then press ENTER.

   This internal loop-back test should give you four replies if TCP/IP is bound to the adapter.

4. To test TCP/IP connectivity with the Instructor computer, type **ping 131.107.2.200** (or an address provided by your instructor) and then press ENTER.

   Four "Reply from 131.107.2.200" messages should appear.

5. Try pinging other computers in your classroom. Recall that IP addresses are assigned as $w.x.y.z$, where $w.x.y$ is exactly the same as in your own IP address, and the remainder, z, is unique to each student's system.

6. To verify TCP/IP parameters for your computer, type **ipconfig /all** and then press ENTER.

The TCP/IP configuration information appears. It should look similar to the information shown in the following two tables.

Windows NT IP configuration

Host name	BDCServer1
DNS servers	131.107.2.200
Node type	Hybrid
NetBIOS scope ID	
IP routing enabled	No
WINS proxy enable	No
NetBIOS resolution	No

Ethernet adapter IEEPRO1

Description	Intel EtherExpress PRO
Physical address	00-AA-00-61-3D-BE
DHCP enabled	Yes
IP address	131.107.2.150
Subnet mask	255.255.255.0
Default gateway	
DHCP server	
Primary WINS server	
Secondary WINS server	
Lease obtained	
Lease expires	

Exercise 3 *(optional)*
Automatically Configuring TCP/IP on a Computer Running Windows NT 4.0

In this exercise, you will configure your computer running Windows NT Server to obtain its IP addressing information from a DHCP server, and then view the addressing information supplied to your computer by the DHCP server.

Note This exercise must not be attempted in the classroom or lab without explicit instructions from the instructor. A DHCP server must be configured prior to the exercise, and it may not conflict with another DHCP server on the network nor issue duplicate addresses to those used on the network. Incorrect implementation of a DHCP server can be seriously disruptive to a network.

➤ **To automatically configure TCP/IP by using DHCP**

In this procedure, you will configure your computer running Windows NT Server to use DHCP to obtain a TCP/IP address.

1. Right-click **Network Neighborhood**, then click **Properties**.

   The **Network** dialog box appears.

2. Click the **Protocols** tab, click **TCP/IP Protocol**, and then click **Properties**.

3. Click the **IP Address** tab, and then click **Obtain an IP address from a DHCP server**.

   A **Microsoft TCP/IP** dialog box appears, indicating that the DHCP protocol will attempt to automatically configure the computer during system initialization.

4. Click **Yes**.

5. Click **OK** to close the **Microsoft TCP/IP Properties** dialog box, and then click **OK** to close the **Network** dialog box.

➤ **To verify the DHCP configuration**

In this procedure, you will verify the Windows NT Server configuration of TCP/IP from the DHCP server.

1. Switch to a Command Prompt.

2. To test TCP/IP connectivity with the Instructor computer, type
ping 131.107.2.200 (or the IP address provided by your instructor) and
then press ENTER.

Four "Reply from 131.107.2.200" messages should appear.

Note If you did not receive four successful replies, contact your instructor.

---

3. To verify the DHCP-assigned TCP/IP parameters for your computer, type
ipconfig /all and then press ENTER.

The TCP/IP configuration information appears. It should look similar to the
information shown in the following two tables.

Windows NT IP configuration

Host name	server1
DNS servers	131.107.2.200
Node type	Hybrid
NetBIOS scope ID	
IP routing enabled	No
WINS proxy enable	No
NetBIOS resolution	No

Ethernet adapter IEEPRO1

Description	Intel EtherExpress PRO
Physical address	00-AA-00-61-3D-BE
DHCP enabled	Yes
IP address	131.107.2.150
Subnet mask	255.255.255.0
Default gateway	
DHCP server	131.107.2.200
Primary WINS server	131.107.2.200
Secondary WINS server	
Lease obtained	Wednesday, July 17, 1998 12:35:00 PM
Lease expires	Tuesday, August 05, 1998 1:31:48 PM

What is the IP address that the DHCP server assigned to your computer?

What is the IP address of the DHCP server?

Lab 5: Documenting the Network

Objectives

After completing this lab, you will be able to:

- Document the network topology used in the classroom.

Estimated time to complete this lab: 10 minutes

Exercise 1
Documenting the Network

This is a pencil-and-paper exercise in which you will learn what network topology has been installed in your classroom. Complete the table below based on information provided to you by your instructor.

Answers recorded in the table will vary for each student.

Network architecture*
Cable type
Connection to network adapter card**
Terminator resistance (Ω ohms)
Impedance (Ω ohms)
Maximum cable segment length
Maximum connected segments
Maximum computers per segment

* Network Architecture: Ethernet 10Base2, Ethernet 10Base5, Ethernet 10BaseT, Ethernet 100BaseT, Ethernet 100BaseVG, Token-Ring, ArcNet, etc.

** Connection Type: RJ45, BNC, etc.

Lab 6: Windows NT 4.0 Hardware Qualifier

Objectives

After completing this lab, you will be able to:

- Test a computer for hardware compatibility with Windows NT 4.0.
- Compare hardware configuration with the Hardware Compatibility List.

Before You Begin

You will need one high-density floppy disk to complete this lab.

NT Hardware Qualifier

NT Hardware Qualifier (NTHQ) is included on the Windows NT installation compact disc. NTHQ is a utility that identifies the hardware installed on a computer. Because NTHQ identifies all detected hardware, it can help troubleshoot installation and boot problems. NTHQ is installed on a Microsoft MS-DOS®-formatted floppy disk, which is then used to boot the system. NTHQ is available only for Intel *x*86–based computers.

Estimated time to complete this lab: 20 minutes

Exercise 1
Creating a Windows NT Hardware Qualifier (NTHQ) Disk

In this exercise, you will create the NTHQ disk.

Note: The NTHQ program is provided on the Windows NT Server 4.0 CD-ROM. If you have the Server installation CD and a CD-ROM drive, you may use it to install NTHQ. Otherwise, connect to your Instructor's shared directory as explained below.

➤ **To create the NTHQ disk**

1. Log on as Student*x*.

2. Use Network Neighborhood to connect to **\\Instructor1\Support**.

3. Insert the high-density floppy disk in drive A.

Note Either a formatted or unformatted disk may be used. The NTHQ program will overwrite any files currently on the disk.

4. Locate the **\Support\HQTool** directory on Instructor1.

5. Run the **Makedisk.bat** program.

Exercise 2
Determining Compatibility with NTHQ

In this exercise, you will use the NTHQ disk to verify the compatibility of your computer to Microsoft Windows NT Server 4.0.

➤ **To run the NTHQ program**

1. Verify that the NTHQ disk made in Exercise 1 is inserted in Drive A.

2. Click the **Start** menu, select **Shutdown**, and choose **Restart the Computer**. The **Hardware Query Tool 4.0 for Windows** dialog box appears.

3. Read the message contained in the dialog box, then click **Yes**.

4. The **Detection Method - comprehensive or safe** dialog box appears. Read the message, then click **Yes**.

5. NTHQ runs in comprehensive detection mode.

6. Explore the results reported for your computer by NTHQ. Use the following table to enter the values for each of the listed hardware components. You will need to click buttons at the bottom of the dialog box in order to display some of the information.

Answers recorded in the table will vary for each student.

Hardware component	Value
Computer system name	
Model	
System revision	
Microprocessor type	
BIOS vendor	
BIOS date	
System bus type	
Network device	
Network device IRQ	
Hard-disk controller device	
Video display device	

7. Compare the list of information you gathered from NTHQ to the Hardware Compatibility List (HCL). The HCL is located in the Support folder of the Microsoft Windows NT Server 4.0 compact disk.

8. Exit the NT Hardware Qualifier program and remove the NTHQ disk from your computer.

9. Restart the computer as a Windows NT 4.0 Server.

Lab 7: Creating User Accounts

Objectives

After completing this lab, you will be able to:

- Create user accounts.
- Create home folders for user accounts.
- Set logon hours restrictions.
- Set account restrictions.
- Test a user account.

Estimated time to complete this lab: 30 minutes

Exercise 1
Creating User Accounts

In this exercise, you will create your user account for the Classroom domain.

This exercise is structured so that you first create accounts and then modify the properties of an account.

Important   The user accounts that you create must be unique to your domain's directory database. If the instructions given in this exercise would result in two or more students with the same user account name, add a number to the end of each of the similar names, such as MNguyen1 and MNguyen2.

➤   **To create a new user account**

1. Log on to your domain (Classroom1, or the domain name provided to you by your instructor) as Administrator.

2. Click **Start,** point to **Programs**, point to **Administrative Tools (Common)**, and then click **User Manager for Domains**.

3. On the **User** menu, click **New User**.

   The **New User** dialog box appears.

4. Configure the following options based on the instructions shown below.

   - **Username** (Enter your name in the form FLastname, where you enter your first initial and first letter of your last name in capital letters, and the remainder of the characters in lower-case letters. Please see the note, above.)

   - **Full Name** (Enter your full name, such as Mai Nguyen.)

   - **Description** (Enter a short phrase to describe yourself, such as Computer Networking Major.)

   - **Password** (Use the word **password**. Passwords are case-sensitive. Please do not enter any other password so that if you are having trouble with your account, your instructor will be able to assist you.)

   - **Confirm Password** (Type **password** again in lower-case letters.)

5. Select the password options indicated below, using your mouse to enter or remove a checkmark from the check box.

   - Clear the checkmark from **User Must Change Password at Next Logon**.

   - Click to add a checkmark in **User Cannot Change Password**.

   - Click to add a checkmark in **Password Never Expires**.

   - Do not add a checkmark to **Account Disabled**.

6. Click **Add**.

   The **New User** dialog box reappears and is cleared so that you can add another user.

7. Click **Cancel** to close the **New User** dialog box.

Exercise 2
Modifying User Accounts

➤   **To create a home folder**

Note Complete this procedure for each user account.

1. In the User Manager for Domains window, double-click your user account.
2. In the **User Properties** dialog box, click **Profile**.
3. In the **Connect** box, click **Z**: so that drive Z will be used to connect to the user's home folder.
4. In the **To** box, type **\\Instructor1\users\%username%** (Instructor1 is the name of the PDC for the classroom domain, and %username% is a special variable that will enter your account's user name as the name of the home directory).

Note In the classroom setup completed by your instructor prior to class, the \Users folder was created and shared on the PDC. In an actual working situation, you would also need to create and share a folder on a volume for this procedure to work.

5. Click **OK** to return to the **User Properties** dialog box.
6. Click **OK** to return to the User Manager window.

➤   **To set logon hours restrictions**

Note Complete this procedure for your own account.

1. In the **User Properties** dialog box, click **Hours**.

   Notice that the default is to allow the user to log on to the network 24 hours a day, 7 days a week.

2. To restrict a user's logon hours, select the appropriate block of time, and then click **Disallow**. To enable a user's logon hours, select the block of time and then click **Allow**.

   - Using your mouse, click on the top left corner and drag to the bottom right corner of the logon hours. Click **Disallow**.

   - Again using your mouse, click on the starting day and time for your class and drag to the ending time for the class, then click **Allow**. Repeat this procedure for each day and time the class meets.

   - For more information about using the **Logon Hours** box, click **Help**.

3. Click **OK**.

➤ **To set the account restriction**

Note Complete this procedure for each user whose account needs to expire.

---

1. In the **User Properties** dialog box, click **Account**.

   Notice that the default option for **Account Expires** is **Never**. The default **Account Type** is **Global Account**.

2. Click **End of**, and then type the date for the end of your class.

3. Click **OK**.

Exercise 3
Testing the New User Accounts

In this exercise, you see that the accounts and home directories were created, and test the account.

➤ **To determine that home folders were created**

1. Use Network Neighborhood to locate **Instructor1**, the computer name for your instructor's computer.

2. Double-click on the icon for Instructor1 to show the shared directories for that system.

3. Double-click on the D:\Winnt\Users folder to display the user's folders.

4. Compare the folders in D:\Winnt\Users with the list of users created for your class; each class member show have a home directory.

Are there any differences?

_____

5. Click **Start,** point to **Programs**, point to **Administrative Tools (Common)**, and then click **User Manager for Domains** to open the dialog box.

6. Compare the folders D:\Winnt\Users with the list of user account names in User Manager for Domains.

What are the differences?

_____

➤ **To test logon hours restrictions**

1. Attempt to log on using the account you created for your name.

2. For the password, enter **PASSWORD**.

Were you able to log on successfully? Why or why not?

_____

3. Attempt to log on again, using **password** as the password entry.

Were you able to log on successfully? Why or why not?

_____

_____

Lab 8: Disabling and Deleting a User Account

Objectives

After completing this lab, you will be able to:

- Disable a user account.
- Delete a user account.

Estimated time to complete this lab: 10 minutes

Exercise 1
Adding a Temporary User Account

In this exercise, you will create and then delete a user account for the Classroom domain. This exercise is structured so that you first create the account, then disable it, and finally delete the account.

➤ **To create the new user account**

1. Log on to your domain (Classroom1, or the domain name provided to you by your instructor) as Administrator.

2. Click **Start,** point to **Programs**, point to **Administrative Tools (Common)**, and then click **User Manager for Domains**.

3. On the **User** menu, click **New User**.

   The **New User** dialog box appears.

4. Configure the following options based on the instructions shown below.

   • **Username** (Enter **Temp-Account***x*, where *x* is the student number you were assigned for this class.)

   • **Full Name** (Enter Temporary Account *x*.)

   • **Description** (No entry is necessary.)

   • **Password** (Use the word **password**. Passwords are case-sensitive. Please do not enter any other password so that if you are having trouble with your account, your instructor will be able to assist you.)

   • **Confirm Password** (Type **password** again in lower-case letters.)

5. Click **Add**.

   The **New User** dialog box reappears and is cleared so that you can add another user.

6. Click **Cancel** to close the **New User** dialog box.

Exercise 2
Testing then Disabling the Temporary User Account

Using the account you just added to the domain, you will first log on to the account to test that it is working, then, after logging off, you will delete the account.

➤ **To Log on using Temp-Account*x***

1. First, log off as Administrator.

   - Press CTRL-ALT-DELETE to display the **Windows NT Security** dialog box.
   - Click **Logoff...** to log off as Administrator.

2. Log on as Temp-Account*x*.

   - When the **Begin Logon** dialog box reappears, press CTRL-ALT-DELETE to display the **Logon Information** dialog box.
   - Type **Temp-Account*x*** as the User name and press TAB.
   - Type **password** as the Password and press ENTER or click **OK**.

   You should now be logged on as the Temp-Account*x* user. If this does not work, repeat the steps above or ask your instructor for help. If you are having difficulty, remember to check the spelling of the User name; although it is not case-sensitive, the specific characters must be typed correctly, including the hyphen included in the name and the numerical digits at the end of the name. Also, remember that the password is case-sensitive and must be typed as **password** in lower-case letters.

➤ **To disable the temporary account**

1. First, log off as Temp-Account*x*.

   - Press CTRL-ALT-DELETE to display the **Windows NT Security** dialog box.
   - Click **Logoff...** to log off.

2. Log on as Administrator.

   - When the **Begin Logon** dialog box reappears, press CTRL-ALT-DELETE to display the **Logon Information** dialog box.
   - Type **Administrator** as the User name and press TAB.
   - Type **password** as the Password and press ENTER or click **OK**.

3. Click **Start,** point to **Programs**, point to **Administrative Tools (Common),** and then click **User Manager for Domains**.

4. From the list of users, double-click **Temp-Account*x*** to select this user account and display its properties.

5. In the **User Properties** dialog box, click the check box for **Account Disabled**.

6. What happens when you log off as Administrator and attempt to log on as **Temp-Account**x?

_____

_____

_____

7. Log on again as Administrator.

8. Click **Start,** point to **Programs**, point to **Administrative Tools (Common)**, and then click **User Manager for Domains**.

9. From the list of users, double-click **Temp-Account**x to select this user account and display its properties.

10. In the **User Properties** dialog box, click the check box for **Account Disabled** to re-enable the account.

11. Test the account. First, log off as Administrator.

12. Log on as Temp-Account*x*.

13. What happens this time when you attempt to log on as Temp-Account*x*?

_____

_____

Exercise 3
Deleting the Temporary User Account

➤ **To delete Temp-Account***x*.

1. First, log off as Temp-Account*x*.

    - Press CTRL-ALT-DELETE to display the **Windows NT Security** dialog box.

    - Click **Logoff...** to log off.

2. Log on as Administrator.

    - When the **Begin Logon** dialog box reappears, press CTRL-ALT-DELETe to display the Logon Information dialog box.

    - Type **Administrator** as the User name and press TAB.

    - Type **password** as the Password and press ENTER or click **OK**.

3. Click **Start,** point to **Programs**, point to **Administrative Tools (Common)**, and then click **User Manager for Domains**.

4. From the list of users, click **Temp-Account***x* to select this user account.

5. On the **User** menu, click **Delete**.

6. What happens when you log off as Administrator and attempt to log on as Temp-Account*x*?

    _____

    _____

Lab 9: Using Diagnostic Utilities

Objectives

After completing this lab, you will be able to:

- Create a real-time Performance Monitor chart.
- Record data for analysis in a Performance Monitor log file.
- Summarize performance data in a Performance Monitor report.
- Install Network Monitor Tools and Agent.
- Use Network Monitor to capture and display network traffic.

Estimated time to complete this lab: 60 minutes

Exercise 1
Creating a Real-Time Performance Monitor Chart

In this exercise, you will create a chart in Performance Monitor to display performance data in real time. Real-time charts provide a quick overview of the current performance of your system.

➤ **To configure the chart**

1. Click the **Start** button, point to **Programs**, point to **Administrative Tools (Common)**, and then click **Performance Monitor**.

2. On the **View** menu, click **Chart**.

3. On the **Edit** menu, click **Add To Chart....**

   Notice that **Processor** is the default object.

4. In the **Counter** list, click **%DPC Time**, and then click **Explain>>**.

   Notice that the **Counter Definition** appears at the bottom of the window.

5. Click each of the counters for the **Processor** object and read the **Counter Definition** for each.

6. In the **Counter** box, select all the counters available for **Processor**, and then click **Add**.

7. Click **Done**.

   A graph appears, displaying the real-time activities for the processor.

➤ **To generate data and view it on the chart**

1. Click the **Start** button, point to **Programs**, point to **Accessories**, point to **Games**, and then click **Pinball**.

2. Play one ball (and *only* one ball) of Pinball.

3. Close Pinball, and then switch to Performance Monitor.

4. In the list of counters, click **% Processor Time**, and notice the changing **Average** value.

Tip To highlight the selected counter, press CTRL+H

---

5. Minimize Performance Monitor.

6. Start and minimize both Server Manager and Disk Administrator.

7. Close both Server Manager and Disk Administrator.

8. Restore Performance Monitor.

9. Notice the activity on the chart, such as spikes.

You have now created a chart displaying real-time processor utilization. This is useful to see how your CPU is being used at the current time. In the next exercise, you will collect and save data for future reference, which can then be turned into a graph to compare with real-time data to analyze performance.

Exercise 2
Recording Data for Analysis in a Performance Monitor Log File

In this exercise, you will use Performance Monitor to create and view a log of processor activity. Logs gather and record data to a file over a period of time. Logs are useful in predicting long-term trends or in troubleshooting short-term problems.

➤ **To create a log**

1. In Performance Monitor, on the **View** menu, click **Log**.
2. On the **Edit** menu, click **Add To Log…**.
3. In the **Objects** list, click **Processor**, and then click **Add**.

Note When you select an object for a log, all counters for that object will be recorded in the log automatically.

---

4. Click **Done**.
5. On the **Options** menu, click **Log…**.
6. In the **File Name** box, type in a name for the log, using your name and a .log extension.

   For example, if your name is Abigail, name your log file Abigail.log.
7. Under **Update Time**, set **Periodic Update Interval** to **1** second.
8. Click **Start Log**.

   The Log window appears, with real-time processor activity being collected in the log.
9. Create processor activity by starting applications or moving the mouse.
10. In Performance Monitor, periodically check the **File Size** box to determine the size of your data file.
11. Wait until the file has reached 100 KB, and then proceed with the next step.
12. On the **Options** menu, click **Log…**, and then click **Stop Log**.

➤   **To view log data in a chart**

1. On the **View** menu, click **Chart**.

2. On the **Options** menu, click **Data From...**.

3. Click **Log File**, and then click the ellipsis (**...**) button.

4. Click the log file that you just created, and then click **Open**.

5. Click **OK** to return to Performance Monitor.

   An empty Chart window appears.

6. On the **Edit** menu, click **Add To Chart**.

7. Select all counters available for **Processor**, and then click **Add**.

8. Click **Done**.

The chart displays the processor counters collected in your log during the log-collection period. You will notice data displayed on the chart as well as on the status bar. The **Last**, **Average**, **Minimum**, and **Maximum** values are displayed with the total graph time from your log of data.

Exercise 3
Summarizing Performance Data in a Performance Monitor Report

In this exercise, you will view portions of the data in a chart to isolate specific information. You will also use reports to view data in a nongraphical format.

➤ **To view isolated segments of log data in a chart**

1. In the list of counters, click **% Processor Time**.

2. Using information from the status bar, record the value for **Average of % Processor Time**.

   _____

3. On the **Edit** menu, click **Time Window...**.

   The **Input Log File Timeframe** dialog box appears. This dialog box contains a slider that is used to adjust the portion of the chart that is shown in Performance Monitor. By default, the entire chart is shown.

   Note You may need to move the Input Log File Timeframe window to see the entire chart.

4. Click the left section of the slider, drag this section to the middle of the bar, and then click **OK**.

   The right half of the original chart is now displayed in Performance Monitor.

5. Record the value for **Average of % Processor Time** again.

   _____

6. Repeat Steps 3 and 4, this time adjusting the slider so that the last one-quarter of the chart is displayed.

7. Record the value for **Average of % Processor Time** again.

   _____

8. Repeat Steps 3 and 4, adjusting the left and right sections of the sliding bar as necessary, until the **Average of % Processor Time** for the portion of the chart displayed in Performance Monitor is greater than 40 percent.

   In your opinion, how accurate is this representation of the processor's use?

   _____

9. Edit the Time window to view the entire graph.

➤   **To create a report showing the % Processor Time for the entire graph period**

1. On the **View** menu, click **Report**.

    A blank Report window appears.

2. On the **Edit** menu, click **Add To Report....**

3. With **Processor** as the default object, in the **Counter** list, select all counters, and then click **Add**.

4. Click **Done**.

    A report with the chosen counters is displayed, showing the averages.

5. What was the average **% Processor Time** for the entire graph period?

    _____

6. Close Performance Monitor.

Exercise 4
Installing Network Monitor Tools and Agent

In this exercise, you will install Network Monitor Tools and Agent.

➤ **To install Network Monitor Tools and Agent**

1. Right-click **Network Neighborhood**, then click **Properties**.

2. Click the **Service**s tab.

3. Click **Add...**.

4. In the **Network Service** box, click **Network Monitor Tools and Agent**, and then click **OK**.

5. In the **Windows NT Setup** dialog box, type **\\instructor1\ntsrv** and then click **Continue**.

   Windows NT Setup copies the required files.

6. After the files have been copied, click **Close**.

7. When prompted, click **Yes** to shut down and restart Windows NT Server.

Exercise 5
Capturing Data with Network Monitor

In this exercise, you will use Network Monitor to capture and display network traffic.

➤ **To set a trigger**

1. Log on as Administrator.

2. Click the **Start** button, point to **Programs**, point to **Administrative Tools (Common)**, and then click **Network Monitor**.

   The Network Monitor Capture window appears.

3. On the **Capture** menu, click **Trigger**.

   The **Capture Trigger** dialog box appears.

4. Under **Trigger on**, click **Buffer Space**.

5. Under **Buffer Space**, click **50%**.

6. Under **Trigger Action**, click **Stop Capture**, and then click **OK**.

➤ **To capture network data and generate network traffic**

1. On the **Capture** menu, click **Start**.

2. On your desktop, click the **Start** button, and then click **Run**.

3. In the **Open** box, type **\\instructor1** and then click **OK**.

   A list of resources on \\Instructor1 appears.

4. In the Instructor window, double-click **Ntsrv**.

➤ **To view network data statistics**

1. Switch to Network Monitor.

2. On the **Capture** menu, click **Stop**.

3. On the **Capture** menu, click **Display Captured Data**.

4. Scroll through the list of captured frames. You should see your own computer name (**server**x) and **instructor1**. You may also see other computer names if those computers were communicating with your server during the capture.

5. Close Network Monitor.

6. Close both the Ntsrv on Instructor1 and Instructor1 windows.

Lab 10: Sharing Folders

Objectives

After completing this lab, you will be able to:

- Share a folder.
- Assign shared folder permissions to users and groups.
- Connect to a shared folder.
- Stop sharing a folder.

Estimated time to complete this lab: 30 minutes

Exercise 1
Sharing Folders

In this exercise, you will share folders and assign permissions.

➤ **To share a folder**

1. Log on as Administrator, and start Windows NT Explorer.
2. Create a folder named **Public** at the root directory level of drive C.
3. Right-click the newly created **Public** folder to display the menu and select the **Properties** option.
4. Click the **Sharing** tab.

Tip When you right-click the Public folder, notice that the **Sharing** command appears on the shortcut menu. If you click **Sharing** on this menu, you will switch directly to the **Sharing** tab of the **Public Properties** dialog box.

---

5. Click **Shared As**.

Notice that the **Share Name** defaults to the name of the folder.

6. In the **Comment** box, type **Shared Public Folder** and then click **OK**.

Looking at Windows NT Explorer, what appears on the Public folder, indicating that it is shared?

Exercise 2
Assigning Shared Folder Permissions

In this exercise, you will determine the current permissions for a shared folder, and assign shared folder permissions to groups in the default domain and to a global group in a different domain.

➤ **To determine the current permissions for the Public shared folder**

1. In Windows NT Explorer, right-click the Public folder, and then click **Sharing**.

    The **Public Properties** dialog box appears.

2. Click **Permissions…**.

    The **Access Through Share Permissions** dialog box appears.

    What are the default permissions for the Public shared folder?

    _____

➤ **To remove permissions for a group**

■ In the **Access Through Share Permissions** dialog box, under **Names**, make sure **Everyone** is selected, and then click **Remove**.

➤ **To assign Full Control permission to the Administrators group**

1. In the **Access Through Share Permissions** dialog box, click **Add…**.

    The **Add Users and Groups** dialog box appears.

    What domain name appears in the **List Names From** box?

    _____

2. Under **Names**, click **Administrators**, and then click **Add**.

    What appears in the **Add Names** box to indicate the location of the directory database where the selected name resides?

    _____

3. In the **Type Of Access** box, select **Full Control**, and then click **OK**.

    The **Access Through Share Permissions** dialog box reappears. Notice that the Administrators group has Full Control permission.

➤ **To assign Read Control permission to the Users group**

1. In the **Access Through Share Permissions** dialog box, click **Add...**.

   The **Add Users and Groups** dialog box appears.

2. Under **Names**, click **Users**, and then click **Add**.

3. In the **Type Of Access** box, select **Read**, and then click **OK**.

   The **Access Through Share Permissions** dialog box reappears. Notice that the Users group has Read permission.

Exercise 3
Connecting to a Shared Folder

In this exercise, you will use two methods to connect to a shared folder. You will then use **Connect as** to specify a different user account to connect to a shared folder.

➤ **To connect to a network drive using the Run command**

1. Click **Start**, and then click **Run**.
2. In the **Open** box, type **\\instructor1** (where x is the number assigned to the instructor's computer) and then click **OK**.

   The Instructor1 window appears.

   Notice that only the folders that are shared appear to network users.
3. Close the Instructor1 window.

➤ **To connect a network drive to a shared folder using Map Network Drive**

1. On the desktop, right-click **Network Neighborhood**, and then click **Map Network Drive**.
2. In the **Drive** box, click **P**.
3. In the **Path** box, type **\\instructor1\public**
4. Clear the **Reconnect at Logon** check box, and then click **OK**.
5. Close the **Public on 'Instructor1'** window.
6. Start Windows NT Explorer and view the drives under My Computer.

   Notice that the directory has been added as Public on 'Instructor1.'

   What drive letter was assigned to the mapped \\Instructor1\Public directory?

➤ **To disconnect a network drive using Windows NT Explorer**

1. In Windows NT Explorer, right-click the drive assigned to \\Instructor1\Public.
2. Click **Disconnect**.

   The drive is removed from the left pane of Windows NT Explorer.
3. Exit Windows NT Explorer and log off.

Exercise 4
Stopping a Shared Folder

In this exercise, you will stop sharing a shared folder.

➤ **To stop sharing a folder**

1. Log on to your domain as Administrator, and then start Windows NT Explorer.

2. Locate and right-click the **Public** folder, and then click **Sharing**.

   The **Sharing** tab of the **Public Properties** dialog box appears.

3. Click **Not Shared,** and then click **OK**.

   Notice that the hand no longer appears on the **Public** folder.

Lab 11: Locating Internet Resources

Objectives

After completing this lab, you will be able to:

- Locate Microsoft Support on-line.
- Use ftp to access and retrieve a file on-line.
- Locate Microsoft TechNet on-line.

Estimated time to complete this lab: 30 minutes

Exercise 1
Locating Microsoft Support Online

In this exercise, you will use the Internet to access Microsoft Support online.

➤ **To locate Microsoft Support online**

1. Log on as Administrator, and start Microsoft Internet Explorer.

   Note   To use the Internet, your system's IP address must be correct for network access through the Internet, you must have a gateway IP address, and the DNS entry must be completed. Because this is unique to each location, the specific information required and the procedure for completing your TCP/IP specifications will be given to you by your instructor.

2. In the address line, type the URL http://www.microsoft.com/support and press ENTER.

3. Click **Support Online** to go to the online support page.

   Note   You may also get to this same page by entering the URL http://support.microsoft.com/

4. In list box number 1 on this page, select the product Windows NT Server

5. In list box number 2 on this page, type **Windows NT Diagnostics** and click the **find** button.

6. When the system responds with a list of articles, browse the articles. Select one of interest to you and click that article to display its contents.

7. Return to the Search Support Online page and type the following search question: **How to troubleshoot basic TCP/IP problems**

8. Click **find**.

9. You may find a title, **How to troubleshoot basic TCP/IP problems in Windows NT 4.0**, in your list. Click this entry to display the result of your search.

10. If you have found the referenced article, you will notice that it contains several potential solutions to TCP/IP problems.

11. Return to the Search Support Online page to enter other searches, or to search for articles suggested by your instructor.

12. Follow the wizard by making selections as indicated. Try different combinations of responses.

13. If a printer is available on your network, print the information.

14. Return to the Search Support Online page to enter other searches, or to search for articles suggested by your instructor.

Exercise 2
Using ftp to Retrieve an File

In this exercise, you will access Microsoft's ftp site, search for an appropriate file, and download it to your system.

➤ **To attach to Microsoft's ftp site via Internet Explorer**

1. In Windows Internet Explorer's address area, type ftp://ftp.microsoft.com and press ENTER.

   The FTP at ftp.microsoft.com windows appears.

2. Click on **dirmap.htm** or **dirmap.txt**. (the first is a hypertext file, the second a text file) and read the instructions to guide you in using the ftp site. The dirmap.htm file contains links to subdirectories; if you use the text file, you will have to return to the initial page to click subdirectories.

3. Click the **Services** directory and then click **TechNet** in the ftp directory list, or click **TechNet in Services** portion of the hypertext dirmap.htm file.

4. Click the README.TXT file to learn about TechNet and see what is available on this site.

5. Return to the root directory of the ftp site.

6. Click **bussys**, then **WinNT**, then **Papers** to reach the site:
   ftp://ftp.microsoft.com/bussys/winnt/winnt-docs/papers/

7. Click the README.TXT file to learn which files are in this directory.

➤ **To attach to Microsoft's ftp site via ftp command**

1. Click **Start**, **Programs**, and select the **Command Prompt** to open a command prompt window.

2. Type **cd ** to make the root directory the default directory. You may also select another directory, such as \temp, for this operation. The purpose of this step is to set a directory as default so that files downloaded from the ftp site are placed into it.

3. At the command prompt, type **ftp ftp.microsoft.com** and press ENTER.

4. The dialog box should show

   C:\>ftp ftp.microsoft.com
   Connected to ftp.microsoft.com.
   220 ftp Microsoft FTP Service (Version 3.0).
   User (ftp.microsoft.com:(none)):

5. At the User prompt, type **anonymous** and press ENTER.

6. For the password, type **AATP-Student** and press ENTER. (At an anonymous ftp site, the normal protocol is to type your e-mail account.) The entry for the password will not be displayed on the screen. The window should now show a listing such as:

User (ftp.microsoft.com:(none)): anonymous

331 Anonymous access allowed, send identity (e-mail name) as password.

Password:

230-This is FTP.MICROSOFT.COM

230-Please see the dirmap.txt file for

230-more information. An alternate

230-location for Windows NT Service

230-Packs is located at:

230-ftp://198.105.232.37/fixes/

230 Anonymous user logged in.

7. Type **cd \bussys\winnt\winnt-docs\papers** and press ENTER.

8. At the ftp prompt, type **dir** and press ENTER to display the content of this directory. These two steps will result in a listing such as:

```
ftp> cd \bussys\winnt\winnt-docs\papers
250 CWD command successful.
ftp> dir
200 PORT command successful.
150 Opening ASCII mode data connection for /bin/ls.
---------- 1 owner   group       699117 Sep 14  1995 ADVNTAGE.EXE
---------- 1 owner   group       184569 Nov  9  1995 CLUSTRWP.EXE
---------- 1 owner   group        36726 Sep 26  1995 DATA_INT.EXE
---------- 1 owner   group       156415 Sep  6  1995 DCE.EXE
---------- 1 owner   group      1000655 Aug 17  1995 DHCPWINS.EXE
---------- 1 owner   group      1218320 Oct 16  1996 DNSWP.EXE
---------- 1 owner   group       278777 Aug 21  1995 DS_STRAT.EXE
---------- 1 owner   group       831270 Aug 23  1995 DSMNGD.EXE
---------- 1 owner   group       574214 Sep 18  1995 FPNW_REV.EXE
---------- 1 owner   group       308383 Sep  8  1995 NT4UNIX.EXE
---------- 1 owner   group       501828 Aug 15  1995 NTENGSCI.EXE
---------- 1 owner   group       428571 Aug 17  1995 Nwipnts.exe
---------- 1 owner   group       420864 Oct 19  1994 RAID0&5.DOC
---------- 1 owner   group        43636 Oct 19  1994 RAID0&5.ZIP
---------- 1 owner   group       526927 Aug 17  1995 RASPAPER.EXE
---------- 1 owner   group        88605 Oct 24  1995 RATINGS.EXE
---------- 1 owner   group         2585 Apr 23  1997 readme.TXT
```

----------	1 owner	group	105071	Oct 23	1995	SERVMAC.EXE
----------	1 owner	group	260234	Jan 23	2:29	TCPIMP2.EXE
----------	1 owner	group	217020	Oct 3	1995	TCPIPIMP.EXE
----------	1 owner	group	1920512	Jan 6	1997	TCPIPIMP2.doc
----------	1 owner	group	126198	Apr 6	1995	UNIXINT.EXE
----------	1 owner	group	1064448	Oct 16	1996	WINSWP.doc
----------	1 owner	group	30316	Sep 6	1995	WISE.EXE

226 Transfer complete.
1727 bytes received in 0.44 seconds (3.92 Kbytes/sec)
226 Transfer complete.
1727 bytes received in 0.44 seconds (3.92 Kbytes/sec)

9. Type **get TCPIPIMP2.DOC** and press ENTER to retrieve a document explaining the implementation of TCP/IP in Windows NT. On your screen, this will produce a display such as:

    ftp> get tcpipimp2.doc
    200 PORT command successful.
    150 Opening ASCII mode data connection for tcpipimp2.doc(1920512 bytes).
    226 Transfer complete.
    1920512 bytes received in 171.47 seconds (11.20 Kbytes/sec)
    ftp>

10. When the transfer completes, type **quit** to exit the ftp command.

    ftp> quit
    221 Thank you for using FTP.MICROSOFT.COM!

    C:\>

11. Type **Exit** to close the command window.

12. Click **Start**, **Programs**, **Accessories**, **WordPad** to open the WordPad application.

13. Click **File**, **Open** and locate the TCPIPIMP2.DOC in the root directory, or in the directory you set as the default.

14. Read the file or close it and read the file at a later time. You may also print the file and/or copy it to a floppy disk to read later.

Exercise 3
Connecting to TechNet

In this exercise, you connect to the Microsoft TechNet Web pages to learn about this subscription support service.

➤ **To connect to TechNet via the Internet**

1. Using the Address space in Windows Internet Explorer, type in the URL **http://www.microsoft.com/technet/** and press ENTER.

2. After reading the TechNet page, click the **TechNet Content** button on the left side of the TechNet window

3. Read the TechNet Content page.

4. At the end of the TechNet Content page, click **Browse Some of the Latest TechNet Articles**.

5. Browse the page, choosing some of the options.

6. Choose **Browse or search a sample of content from the TechNetCD**.

7. Browse the contents of this page.

8. Optionally, and if a printer is available through the network, print an article from Technet.

9. Close Internet Explorer when you have finished browsing the TechNet page.